Leave No Wake

Poems by

Marie Gauthier

In memory of my parents, Reba & Leo

Published by Pine Row Press
Ft. Mitchell, KY 41011

ISBN: 978-1-7363394-4-2

April 2022

First Edition

10 9 8 7 6 5 4 3 2 1

Cover art credit: Heather Rush

Publisher's website at pinerow.com

Author's website at marie-gauthier.com

Leave No Wake

Contents

III.

Acknowledgments

My abiding thanks to the editors of the following publications where these poems first appeared, sometimes in previous forms:

The Adroit Journal: "Four Elements" and "Summer Sundays"

burntdistrict: "Where You Split, You Bloom"

Cave Wall: "Conservationist" and "Little God & His Mother, Act I"

Chronogram: "Aubade"

Clarion: "Labor Day"

Connotation Press: An Online Artifact: "Distinct from Trees"

The Greenfield Recorder: "Death into Life"

The Grove Review: "Diagnosis: Stage IV" and "Recession"

Hunger Mountain: *"Pantala flavescens"*

Iron Horse Literary Review: "Winter Nocturne"

Linebreak: "The Bat"

Literary Mama: "Insomnia"

The MacGuffin: "Repair"

Magma Poetry: "Genesis" and "His Snores"

Other Poetry: "Echolocation"

Pine Row: "'Bomb de terre'" and "December Eclipse"

Poetry Northwest: "Grief Scale"

Redactions: Poetry, Poetics, & Prose: "Elegy"

RHINO Poetry: "The Minor Saints Make Do"

Salamander: "Motherless"

Sugar House Review: "The Fall" and "Vespers"

Tar River Poetry: "Spring Crocuses"

Weave Magazine: "Recondite"

West Review: "The Art of Aging"

Whiskey Island Magazine: "Rerouting the Superhighway"

"All Souls'" and "Plenitude" were awarded a 2008 Dorothy Sargent Rosenberg Poetry Prize, while "Little God & His Mother, Act I" and "Four Elements" received Honorable Mention for the 2010 Dorothy Sargent Rosenberg Poetry Prize.

Some of these poems appeared in a chapbook, *Hunger All Inside*, published by Finishing Line Press in 2009.

Thank you to Jennifer Militello, Ines P. Rivera Prosdocimi, and Enzo Silon Surin, for being so generous and kind and encouraging!

Thank you to my publisher, Hank Hudepohl, for your leap of faith, and to Heather Rush for designing the gorgeous cover! I couldn't be happier or more honored by the marshaling of such talent in service of my poems.

To the poets and friends who've been a part of my literary community—thank you all from the bottom of my heart for your wisdom, words, and fellowship.

Lastly, all my love always to my entire family tree, Gauthiers, Greens, and Groovers, especially Lance and the kids—you sustain and inspire me every day.

I.

"Bomb de terre"
—From a headline in *The Telegraph*

Hand grenades dug up for potatoes
in France—how often do we evade
calamity? Most things can be mistaken
for potatoes in dirt. Clean them up,
most things are still ordinary.
The children color at their stations
after the lockdown drill, lights on,
crisscross applesauce. They keep
their hands to their own bodies.
The marchers wave signs and chant
in unison, arms locked, in lock-step,
safe in numbers. The walk you take ends
at a sunlit café, where you drink
chai, a glass of water, and walk home
again, smelling of cardamom.
Heedless geniuses of the place,
we consult no one and live on, not
even pretending to read the sign,
striding off across new grass.

Insomnia

Often I wake to the sound
of his pacing downstairs, stalking

sleep from room to room, water running
in a glass, dishes clinking in the sink.

Back when I smoked, I'd rise too,
any excuse to glow in the dark.

Late summer nights, I'd kick
my legs over his, nude

beneath my night shirt, letting the tide
of his voice wash over me.

Specters billowed from my cigarette
out the open window, a generously

animate moonlit float
carrying our words as it drifted.

These days, hitched, child-bound,
strapped for time, my sleep

is a noun needing protection.
I pull the covers close

while he stirs his 3am polenta,

spare my feet the sand

on the floor, the memory
of salt in the air.

Labor Day

The living move in long-winded waves
as if through glacial tides
while the slow lathe of the carousel
creaks its send-off to summer.

Horses, gilded dust billowing, eyes
sand-scuffed mother-of-pearl,
bow to the children, to parents
hefting their lithe charges.

Everyone takes their place, hits
their mark, relinquishes their ticket
for this season's last ride, mechanisms
crusted like salt along the bilge.

As the axis cranks piano sweet-talk,
small bodies ease in their saddles.
Smiles alight and flit across their faces:
an astonishing flock of radiance.

Winter Nocturne

You love how snow smudges
the edges of things, how the ice-blue air leans
        into the empty

laps of winter trees—he can hear
the rush, your firstborn, feels frost on his cheeks
        between dreams—

spiders and bats, bats and spiders—
his newest names for fear: shadows hide multitudes,
        and December is all

shadow, a Never Never Land
of night. But you find comfort in the dark, those small
        cold hours whose quiet

amplifies every sound—scratch
and chatter of squirrels in the ceiling, the glottal
        reprise of the baby

sleeping in his crib, the heat's
traveling clank—how it tells you exactly where each
        loved body lies

and will remain until morning.

December Eclipse

Dove-colored damasks
of cloud scud by, soften
the bite of a starlit night,
the antipodes of resolution
and result. Snow falls

in longhand, a desultory
expanse of loops across
an obsidian moon, dark
doppelgänger—the year's
dilating eye.

Solstice

It was December, and we'd decided
not to be in love—
or I'd decided, tired of carrying
that glass egg of hope.

A long night of soft snow,
I held his arm as we marked
a trail on the sidewalk,
the fall of white

a kaleidoscope of shadows
through the streetlights,
what I'd thought I'd wanted
a heavy coat cast off.

Plenitude

1.

I knew at conception—
I blinked, felt twinned—

as you know at once
by your parched tongue

the persimmon
you've bitten isn't ripe.

2.

Some days our boy's
a barnacle
clamped to my breast.

3.

December in Yarmouth:

We crouch on the rocks
of the breakwater

listening to seashells
click at the water's edge,

jostled by the ocean.

The beach teems with periwinkles.
How to go?

Seashells splinter underfoot.

4.

Home: just a block away,
a century-old building
spews smoke. Within minutes
the roof is engulfed with flames,
bricks hurtling
from the cracked veneer.

Firefighters from twelve towns
respond. Four businesses
and three apartments burn.

No fatalities.

Within days the fire is deemed
suspicious, the gutted husk
razed. One week till Christmas,
all the houses are limned
by lights. *Firetrucks!*
Our toddler cries: *Lights!*

5.

He loves the snow, even
when he falls face first.

In the midst of a nor'easter
we trundle, he a red bob

in a sea of white.

He waves and calls *Thank you!*
to every car easing by,

points at each icicle
stretching from the eaves,

laughs at the wind's toss,
its daub of snow on his nose.

Cesarean

Flint, fire, then smolder,
smoky and resinous,

languorous heat sliding
through her veins.

There's a sharpness below
her ribs, a tugging,

her belly a basin
of blood and brine

as the child, gray
as shock, shocked

beyond breath, is lifted
through the rift.

All Souls'

These fall days rife with ghosts,
        he's all apple, my apple, rosy
and full of tart *nos* and *yodel-o's.*

Out, out, he cries each morning,
        so we bundle up, and he barrels
through phalanxes of leaves—

dun-colored, breath-thin,
        they crumple beneath his feet
like letters from the dead,

unearthed too late, or too soon
        for his reading, letters sent
to ones uncaring or careless

or dead now too, that they
        should end as mulch.
The trees reach for him

with gaunt arms—do they grieve
        their lost pages?—cracking as they
bend—but however they beseech,

puckish unassailable he
        merely scuttles away, his ripeness
the only song he hears.

Morning Run

We buried my father before his fiftieth year,
dead in his sleep one summer morning.

I settle into my run, tempering my breath
to a rooted and silent in and out,

My mother eighteen years after.

modulate my tempo till I land lightly
on each quickening foot.

The snow from a March squall
half-melted on the ground.

I'm listening for their deciduous voices,

attempting a seamless passage through the air,
something like a gust, or a ghost, might do.

The Bat

turns up like an artifact
of our early days,
the time one zipped

into your hovel—lacking
kitchen, doors,
a stick of proper furniture—

and you hopped from leg to leg,
your coat a white flag
flapping along the ceiling.

Now there's a boy—
and he's got a whole trove
of darkness and dreads-to-be.

Thus you quash the panic
that bids you *run!* that warns
rabies! that wonders

if it's big enough to carry
off the cat—When it finds
a perch above the back door,

you show our boy how it hangs
upside down, explain
that the bat, like any of us,

just wants a warm bed.
You cup it in gloved hands,
as close as you've ever been

to the bare nose
of a big brown bat, while he
props open the door.

Together you countdown.
Together, you release
the wriggling rocket.

Rerouting the Superhighway

He's pruning the maple,
his handsaw eating the hardwood
until the severed limbs fall.

Our boy watches from the window,
smiling like one promised a chocolate
heart—he knows why

the tree must bear its loss:
squirrels, scores of squirrels, travel
its branches into our ceilings.

Sometimes one, perhaps
the original squirrel, pioneer
of our troubles, perches for minutes

at a time, right by that window.
Tail twitching, it stares,
all cheek and chitter, then

launches itself up, over, and in.
The interminable skittering overhead,
the periodic ruts and animal moans—

the boy wakes crying, carries a stick
to rout them out. At the trunk, our neighbor
gripes about lost shade, lost privacy,

but we couldn't care less: Our rooms brim
with sunshine—golden-warm silence—
dripping like syrup from the eaves.

Psalm 51: Antiphon

Grace falls, a sibilance of snow, curls
tufts among violets you crush.

Grace ferns your cheekbones, pools
in the pillowed hollows of your young son's neck.

Grace in the fretted sting of a mosquito you swat,
the smell of wood smoke and charred fish.

Summer's green skies. The furred scat of coyotes,
the small bones poking through its crust.

Grace, the sharp thrust of air you pass through
on your way to somewhere else.

II.

Recession

Time now to hold our breath
for the season's first snow, its gentle
exultation. We fish pennies
for a tree from the baby's mouth,

let the boy play with flour and water.
Focused, face frozen, he puffs white,
rolling pin chiding the dough flat.
The baby emits cyclic shrieks,

crawling through clouds sifting down
from the table. Books used, clothes used.
Milk in a box good for a year.
Yet how easily they love their lives,

what slight graspable dreams—they skate
the floor through drifts of flour,
while the year's footfalls retreat
through crystallized sheaths of leaves.

Recondite

What you wanted:
Sun-spangled
days, a wind
with bells in it.
You wanted: Better
ancestors, better
angels, for them
to materialize suddenly
like the heron flying over
the highway Easter morning,
legs dangling as if ringed
with silver, as if tied
to a boy unspooling miles
of string. To be tethered
to some fixed star.

Aubade

Before the boy and his early
morning wails— *I'm too big too big*—
as if sleep's dark magic remade him
unknowably giant-sized.

Before the baby and his staccato
sobs, little red body curling
and arching like a snapped rubber band.
Before the sun and its attendant

duties, before the mockingbird's
strident high and low. Before the neighbor's
shoe-clatters above, before traffic,
after love—your breath rumbles

hot in my ear, the bass note
our life is strung upon.

Four Elements

after Gottfried Semper

I. The Plinth

Our son and his friends
build a snow grotto
atop ground unyielding as granite.

Their giggles curl in the wind.
Candy-colored shovels script
against an ice floor—something

accrues with its slick hardening.
It returns to the children, winter
to winter—how to decipher

the handicraft of snow's blue
prints. Deep in their holes,
late potatoes close their eyes.

II. The Wall

Farmers tilled their land and hauled the stones,
harvest of frost heaves, to fence lines.
Barriers to wandering livestock,
markers of possession—field stones, flagstone,
tie stones—extended into lichen-crusted vertebrae:
atlas of a disappearing landscape.

III. The Roof

Never mind the stars. Come
daylight, take the heliotrope's

measure, the sun's glance
mirrored in a vast, exact, arc:

what's needed: precision: somewhere
to start: somewhere to be.

IV. The Hearth

Wool-capped ladies bring winter
apples, and tangerines
in miniature wooden crates.

The bread: A day away from stale.
But food bank boxes burst
with turnips, sweet potatoes,

skins darkly powdered with local
farm dirt, beets bloodstain-brown.
We stow them in an unheated room.

On the stovetop, cocoa melds
with condensed milk in a pot
warming on the burner.

Small economies: how the sun yields
to December, bows to evening
before the end of afternoon.

Pantala flavescens

Day's close—August's ineluctable heat
avows rain, relief. Above the new-mown

meadow, an aria of wings:
the swarm strafes gold.

The swooping orbits catch an updraft—
fluted notes lift, then veer back again.

Forethought, foregone, dragonflies skim
air like fingers on glass, elocutions that shimmer

and rustle, yield and return,
the tablature in ceaseless shift.

Obbligato: mosquito-static, whine—
those raconteurs of zing lead

night's overture, second strings plucked
mid-air and mouthed, off-key.

Desire glides along broken chords, death
but one octave below.

His Snores

They
begin
with a light
whoosh, an almost
imperceptible
stutter snagged in first gear
until the engine stalls—but
the next breath explodes—infernal
crescendo, the damned's gathering rage.

Tinnitis

Banshees shrieking in my cloven head—
gloss of unreal blurs like twilight.
Fever-loud whine for my ears
alone, this chrysalis
burrowed at the nape
creeps to the fore.
Caul-eater—
din that
drowns.

Conservationist

We've rambled deep into snowy
pockets of the woods

when his summons comes
from a clearing: I step into the sun's

bright grasp to where he stands
by an old flagstone foundation, the corpse

of someone's home. Some unknown one,
but he knows the story. Names

dissolve even as they're spoken, dates,
entire conversations plucked like leaves

from his mind's branches, but he always knows
the story, all the workaday heartaches

thrumming at the root. What once seemed
a sad attachment to blight I recognize

as an incantation against forgetting
these vast acres of felled lives,

how small the axe that felled them.

Mulberry

Summer decades past
we played in my grandmother's
backyard boundless

as an unfinished map.
The trees bent low
their limbs heavy

with berries we gleaned
and ate over and over the air
sweet with disbelief.

Our parents smiled from lawn
chairs hands empty save
my mother's cigarette

fixed as a photograph
or my memory of a photograph
bleeding away with time,

a Polaroid in reverse.
We burst the berries
between our teeth spit

the seeds at each other
our parents silently
watching from the shade.

Our fingers red-stained.
Still there was no end
to the berries, the trees.

Repair

The swallows have fled their nests
in the tobacco barn to stitch
sharp angles in the summer sky.

You with your ruined face watch,
finger poised on a word from the book
still in your lap: *memory*.

Loneliness blooms inside you
like the bones of an old umbrella.

Its thin nimbus casts a shadow—a lace
of holes big enough for even you to breach.

Summer Sundays

At the lake, aunts, cousins,
uncles spread
over five picnic tables,
some familial plague.

The sun, exhausted,
slumps off behind the trees.
One last game
of bocce ball, one last

jump from the abandoned
lifeguard's chair.
We feel alien
in our t-shirts & jeans

our burnt skin & coronets
of wind-snarled hair.
Clouds of black flies
clot the cooling

night—we extend
our arms as if we could
catch anything & run.
We run headlong.

Echolocation

The neighbor's daughter practices violin.

    The up and down whine of scales—a fluency

of feeling if not sound—scrolls the courtyard

    with a crow's grace. Its dream-shatter

of flap and caw. At odds with each other,

    we listen. We forget dinner, anger, forget

the nowhere we've abandoned ourselves—

    the music spindles, an infinite metallic coil.

Distinct from Trees

The kindling's caught fire—
your first lament sparks
wild, an electric

flex and spring.
The green pine refuses
to burn.

The sphere of new grief
is the late August sun, cracked
egg bubbling on the hot

skillet, the cross-section
of an umbilical cord, cut
then clamped.

Poise's errata arrives
late, later than now, later than
stars collapsing

your heart.
Next spring, perhaps,
you'll return to these woods,

to the sap's indelible
stamp. But will you ever again
stand as tall?

Little God & His Mother, Act I

She's clover crushed beneath his toes,
his trail of sweet green. When the wind hums

a portamento through the portico
he spins between its pillars,

weathervane of full-fleshed boy, stomps
his rain boots in puddles of sun, on ants

scurrying too late. He kicks their hills
into dust. *Once upon a time*, he says

and tears a page from her book. *I wonder
what you are,* he sings, crumpling the page

in his hands. The words are his, he is the words.
None may know them but he.

Genesis

Arterial-bright, the coast of death.
Estuaries flow through the gates
of history, indeterminate as joy,
the keel of laughter. Mystery's name
is ocean prayer, is question & rupture,
swirl of tide. Urgency. The vast world's
xanthic yolk—zygote.

III.

Diagnosis: Stage IV

Your wings are swelled
       to honeycomb, afflicted
              sacs of marauding cells—

you're more
earthbound than ever.

A vast scattering
       lights up the darkened
              grayscale scan: constellation

whose every new star
steals years from your life.

Years. How can you bear it?
       How will we?
              But there's no lasting

anodyne for this, that, there:
the luminous

hive eclipsing your heart.

The Minor Saints Make Do

Exiled by a muscular god,
the minor saints sleep
upright now, peel oranges

& sunburns. The prophecies
dreamt in kinder climes
absent themselves by increments:

the afterlife has come & gone.
They sing *stone*, sing *stars*—
the old griefs shudder & fall.

Motherless

A quiet nothing like peace,

only the subtraction of sound: breath, heartbeat,

oxygen machine—everything stilled

to this: the sound of sobs in a vacuum.

Her mouth yawns, an airless maw, tongue

slumped to one side like a closed pink

tulip. I lift her jaw and prop it with a pillow,

prop the pillow with her dough-warm hands—

a pantomime of devotion they will

inevitably disturb. Before the body bag,

before the gurney, the hospice nurse and I perform

the ablutions, dress my mother in clean soft cotton.

We six, her children grown, cry in waves.

Each hour rings the loss of her, time emptying

its minutes into the room cavernous

without the hospital bed, the room where my boys,

her youngest grands, spin like lodestones

in a haywire compass, unmoored by its vacancy.

In the living room, my brothers divvy up

their secondhand suits among the family men,

each trying on pants and jackets, passing

what doesn't fit on to the next.

Who has a tie? A tie pin? Shoe polish? Shoes?

Grief Scale

i. Hummingbird at rest.

ii. A letter in the post, rain-damp, belated.

iii. You no longer read the newspaper.

iv. Child touching two fingers to the keys of an upright,
    the felted breath of dissonance.

v. Thunder's approaching bass, trebled against glass.

vi. Inhale a cold muddle of clouds. Frost
    glazes your heart, your gut.

vii. Stasis.

viii. Stasis.

ix. Speak, and speak again, about nothing and no one.

x. Crow wings a wind shear—
    the ice forest creaks and fractures
    into ten thousand tiny knives.

xi. Wrest the bloody shards—
    from your scalp, your hands, the hollows
    beneath your breasts—for the rest of your life.

xii. Bless them all.

Spring Crocuses

Winter is the mother
        chiseled underground,
acres of graves buried by snow.

Cancer beveled her
        to bone; two steps
were too much by the end. I lifted

her onto the borrowed
        bed, cupped her head,
its tamarisk wisps of white.

Her mottled hands clawed
        at the blankets: forty years
in the north, and still

she can't she couldn't
        abide the cold.
She sighed a smile, settling in.

I thought then she'd see
        the spring—do all the dying
sneak out just ahead of the sun?

The crocuses poked along
        days after, late stars
of the lengthening light, useless.

Where You Split, You Bloom

—after Lia Purpura

Your stone's a new milk tooth
among the weathered markers—
how to make of your loss something less
never, less always, less torn
sutures and sawtooth incisions?

Your appointments meant CBCs,
IV lines, the blue stars of radiation.
Mine are heartbeats. Sonograms.
The contrapuntal pulses of the living.

The phlebotomist's smooth ruby draw
pains me beyond galaxies: the memory
of your cigarette paper skin and elusive veins,
how your face charred to ash with each

needle's dig. I press gauze to the red pearl.
The bell of my belly strains and shakes
with each strike of the ringer inside.

Last Bequest

They fit in my hand, the consolations of the leftover
and left behind :: sand from her box of seed pearls,
a rotary dial hole, tacky gold crystals of honey.

I inter memories in remnants :: the beaded heads
of pins, spools of typewriter ribbon, a shift key ::
time-stamped and durable. Find traces of the revenant ::

peach stone, tea leaves, tobacco flecks :: in her compost
and combustibles. Small green buds of unripe grapes
and six milk teeth :: fossils and stars of one life's
    constellation.

Elegy

Each autumn the birds descend
to your grapevines

till the branches are bare.
Without you, their bounty of fruit

grows—as well as their numbers.
The robins look no plumper.

*

Inky beetles scutter
over our anchor

in the casket, who remains
adamantly dead.

*

When the wind disturbs the eaves
I don't hear your voice.

Walking in early evening,
shadows deepen

without any hint of you.

*

I no longer have mornings
of forgetting

you're gone.
The quiet's broken

by rainfall snapping
against the screens

of open windows.
Birdsong. The clap

of my son's small hands.

Ode to Spring

The sky equivocates, one
moment a gray corpse, the next
a risen and glowing Lazarus.

These are the days of layers, days
of lilacs, days of running with glasses
smudged by the rain, the morning air

dense and cool, indicative of nothing.
Days of clear sidewalks, open
windows, window guards, nights

of neighbor sounds keeping you awake.
Mud season's past, its slow reveal
of brown, browner, brownest—

these are the days of longer days,
of bicycles and handstands, the dandelions
and all of us losing our heads.

Grace Note

Summer gives me peonies, lemon
water, the children's sunlit upturned faces.

Newly shorn nearly naked, they torque
their bodies down the grassy hill, bodies

they love, limbs that never fail.
My limber nimble lambs reel with laughter.

When they return dewy and breathless
they flourish one blowsy fuchsia bloom—

A rose! they exclaim. *Almost,* I say. *But a peony
is to a rose as you are to me. Abundance.*

Vespers

Another blushed linen dusk
robins trilling the end of days
crows silent and scarce
for a change
the hymn of the passing train
long since died away
the air warm as breath
animate with clouds
of black flies
moth dust.
You're still
gone.

The Fall

The days are getting warmer, greener, the air alive
with bugs. The teenager who flew down winter
    mountains
shrieks when a hornet lands on his arm's bare skin.

He was stung in the fall clambering on the roof,
    cleaning
leaves out of gutters. Wasps dived at him—
Caterwaul of pain and panic—that's what he
    remembers.

He nearly fell. Only some miracle of luck and instinct
prevented it. It's been days since his friend fell
into a coma—friend of his first kiss, friend who plays

ukulele and ultimate frisbee, gamine girl in tie dye
and flowered dresses marching in Pride. He asks every
    day
if there's news, writes her: *I'm worried about you,*
    worried

that you might die and I debate sending that message,
think of the mother who'll do the reading, the hospital
    room
festooned with prayer flags and sprigs of bleeding
    hearts—

Scattered hornets buzz and bump the skylights,

their nest hidden deep in the chimney.
I sweep winged bodies from the floor when they fall.

The Art of Aging

About menopause they are never wrong,
the old matriarchs: they know the flush
of heat as you burn from the inside out,
how no amount of discarding clothes cools
its fires. How colleagues peer over screens,
ceramic mugs steaming in their hands,
dispensing movie spoilers and cat videos
as if you weren't this minute dissolving
like salt in warm vinegar—granular, gradual.
How inestimably kind the iron-haired cashier
seems with your bananas, while you're invisible
to the tattooed young bagger, hands nail-bitten
thickly veined, tossing everything into your cart—
she knows there's either murder in your heart
or an endless berm and swale of vague
wanderings in search of your last true thought.
Who knows how blood boils and spatters
rather than flows, knows when the tide
crests bloodthirsty—the crones keep mum.

Death to Life

When winter ended,
the bushes hung

so brown and forlorn,
I thought we'd failed them—

more deaths to tally in the ledgers
of moral responsibility—

The missing panicles
of the sumac trees,
more *oracles* than *Heracles*.

The cat that faded in days,
more Cheshire than calico.

The carelessness of all
four parents lost—

But when a friend mentioned hers
hadn't flowered for the first
spring in memory

I began seeing them
everywhere:
leaves of burlap where

there should've been green stars

supernova with blooms.

We found the right person
with the right information
at the dump,

where our distant neighbor
and master gardener
told us: wind killed

the rhododendrons, record
winds and climate change—

more human nature
          than Mother Nature.

We could have spun
that thought to further

conclusions, the acres of death,
imagined all the winters to come.

But the vast incapacitates,
so we turned instead

with the relief of letting go,
relief of being blameless,
or helpless, or hapless

to our neighbor's advice: look
for signs of life, and brook

no weakness—cut it
down to the ground.

Spring Morning

My daughter tip-toe dances on the deck
singing to the birds, the morning light
faint on the boys sipping warm milk—
Chickadee dee dee! She's missing
her two front teeth. Her brothers laugh
every time she laughs. She loves
making them laugh, which makes her,
and them, laugh. The chickadees love
her song. They chirp back, flitting
from branch to branch. In this way
love repeats from our home to the trees,
to the sky, returns to our home to the trees,
to the sky, something we keep and give away.

Johnny-on-the-spot

Rigged out in hard hat,
neon vest and ear plugs,

the worker missed
the radio call—*Deer on site!*

Construction cleaved
the road, a din and disfiguration

of woods to the west
turned cliffside,

so he saw you
before hearing the alarm—

a panicked fawn tearing
through the disarray

straight to danger,
your cry so child-like

past three or four
other confused workers

till he scooped you up
and scrambled towards safety.

His steel-toed boots scrabbled

through the gravel

all the while you struggled
and squirmed,

your bleats reverberating
through the rubber in his ears.

Fawn so new you coated
his arms in afterbirth,

so new you never knew
a home.

Leave No Wake,

but our boat rocks
        too slowly as it is, our dead
                anchors in the inkiest depths.

           Mr. Fancy laments our lack
      of sails, or motor, clucks
and knuckles the wooden hull.

It's Mr. Fancy's boat.
      I pour cocoa from thermos
           to mugs for two of the three kids,

         their laughter bright bells
      over the water that swallows
more land every year—

Its sway is lull as deception,
      rising tide, rising bile—
          their brother begins

          retching over the gunwale,
      convulsive comma hanging on.
He blinks at me, feral

in misery, and I grab
      the oars, row when I'd
         rather hold him, row

as the other two pack up
the basket, wrap him
in a blanket, pat his back.

Mr. Fancy says he's worried
about the boy, vaguely
motioning towards the oars,

the spatter on the wood. His tongue
knocks against his teeth,
What should we do?

Cluck, cluck.
As if I wasn't this very
minute making waves, making

progress, struggling towards
the shrinking shore.

Life After Life

I held them for several
minutes before the shapes
made sense—disembodied

mouse tail, arc and red tissue
not tomato but remains
of a small rib cage—

the cats' leftovers.
The cats now gone, calls
the coyote from the night

woods, the two become
one and then none, life's
inevitable attrition.

What rainbow bridge exists
for mice and unmentionables,
our late lamented felines,

ourselves? The lure of second lives—
do we ever get anything right
the first time? Night hunt, bike ride,

serenade, kiss. The coyote's
stuttering two a.m. solo
wakes me from a dream—

racing downhill on my Huffy,
smoky cats in the basket, my father's
push telling me to fly—

I love all my ghosts, mistake

each for more than an unnamed
wish, some vestigial wing.

Marie Gauthier works as the marketing project editor at Pioneer Valley Books. She is a Franklin County regional representative for Mass Poetry, runs the Collected Poets Series, and is the founding president of the League of Women Voters of Franklin County. She serves on the LWVMA board, and co-chairs the LWVMA Membership Steering Committee. Previously she was the GM at the Jeffery Amherst Bookshop in Amherst, Mass., and Director of Sales & Marketing at Tupelo Press.

Her poems have appeared in many journals, including *The West Review, Linebreak, Cave Wall, Sugar House Review, Hunger Mountain, Crab Creek Review, The Grove Review, Poetry Northwest, The Common*, and elsewhere.

She was the recipient of a 2008 Dorothy Sargent Rosenberg Poetry Prize, and received Honorable Mention in the 2010 Dorothy Prizes. Her chapbook, Hunger All Inside, was released by Finishing Line Press in October 2009.

Marie lives with her family in Shelburne Falls, Mass.

Made in the USA
Middletown, DE
08 April 2022